contents

NZ, Canada, US and UK readers
Please note that Australian cup and
spoon measurements are metric.
A conversion chart appears on page 62.

tapenade and tomato pastries

2 sheets ready-rolled puff pastry
½ cup (60g) seeded black olives
2 teaspoons drained rinsed baby capers
2 teaspoons fresh lemon thyme leaves
2 teaspoons coarsely chopped fresh flat-leaf parsley
2 teaspoons olive oil
2 medium tomatoes (380g), sliced thinly
30g fetta cheese, crumbled
1 tablespoon fresh oregano leaves

1 Preheat oven to 200°C/180°C fan-forced. Line oven tray with baking paper.
2 Cut six 8.5cm rounds from each pastry sheet. Place on tray; using fork, prick rounds five times, cover with baking paper, place another oven tray on top of pastry rounds. Bake, covered with tray, about 10 minutes or until golden brown.
3 Meanwhile, blend or process olives, capers, thyme, parsley and oil until tapenade is just combined.
4 Divide tomato among pastry bases; top each with 1 rounded teaspoon of the tapenade. Sprinkle with cheese and oregano.

serves 4
preparation time 10 minutes
cooking time 10 minutes
per serving 23.3g fat; 1585kJ (379 cal)
tips The oven tray placed on top of the pastry rounds while they're baking is to stop the pastry from puffing. Pastry rounds can be made a day ahead; store them in an airtight container.

gorgonzola and fennel tartlets

120g gorgonzola cheese, crumbled
½ cup (120g) sour cream
2 eggs
1 tablespoon olive oil
2 small fennel (600g), trimmed, halved, sliced thinly
4 sheets fillo pastry
cooking-oil spray

1 Blend or process cheese, sour cream and eggs until smooth; transfer to large jug.
2 Heat oil in small frying pan; cook fennel, stirring, until soft.
3 Preheat oven to 180°C/160°C fan-forced. Lightly oil two 12-hole mini (1 tablespoon/20ml) muffin pans.
4 Cut pastry into 7cm squares. Stack two squares of pastry on board; spray with oil. Place another two squares diagonally on top to make star shape; spray with oil. Press into hole of mini muffin pan; repeat with remaining pastry.
5 Divide cheese mixture among pastry cases; top with fennel. Bake, uncovered, about 15 minutes or until filling sets and pastry is browned lightly. Stand tartlets in pans 5 minutes before serving hot.

makes 24
preparation time 20 minutes
cooking time 20 minutes
per tartlet 5g fat; 254kJ (61 cal)

curry puffs with chutney dip

Unbaked filled curry puffs can be prepared up to a month ahead and frozen in an airtight container. Curry puff filling and chutney dip can be prepared a day ahead. Cover separately; refrigerate until required.

1 tablespoon vegetable oil
2 green onions, chopped finely
1 clove garlic, crushed
2 teaspoons curry powder
300g beef mince
2 teaspoons lemon juice
⅓ cup (110g) mango chutney
4 sheets ready-rolled puff pastry
1 egg, beaten lightly
chutney dip
⅔ cup (220g) mango chutney
1 tablespoon water

1 Heat oil in medium saucepan; cook onion and garlic, stirring, until onion softens. Add curry powder; cook, stirring, until fragrant. Add beef; cook, stirring, until beef is browned and cooked through. Remove from heat; stir in juice and chutney.
2 Using rolling pin, roll each pastry sheet into 30cm square. Using 8cm-round cutter, cut eight rounds from each pastry sheet.
3 Preheat oven to 200°C/180°C fan-forced. Lightly oil two oven trays.
4 Place one heaped teaspoon of the beef mixture on one round; brush edges with a little beaten egg, fold over to enclose filling. Press edges with fork to seal; repeat with remaining beef mixture and pastry.
5 Place curry puffs on oven trays; brush with remaining egg. Bake, uncovered, about 15 minutes or until browned lightly.
6 Serve hot with warm chutney dip.
chutney dip Combine ingredients in small saucepan; stir over low heat until combined.

makes 32
preparation time 40 minutes
cooking time 25 minutes
per curry puff 6.2g fat; 439kJ (105 cal)
per tablespoon chutney 0.1g fat; 179kJ (43 cal)

beef turnovers

1 tablespoon olive oil
2 medium brown onions (300g), chopped coarsely
800g beef mince
2 medium carrots (240g), chopped coarsely
¼ cup plain flour (35g)
3 cups beef stock (750ml)
1½ cups frozen peas (185g)
1 cup frozen corn kernels (140g)
6 sheets ready-rolled puff pastry
1 egg, beaten lightly

1 Heat oil in large heavy-based saucepan; cook onion, stirring, until soft. Add beef; cook, stirring, until beef changes colour. Add carrot, and blended flour and stock; cook, stirring, until mixture boils and thickens. Stir in peas and corn; cool.
2 Cut six 18cm-rounds from pastry. Join pastry scraps; cut two more 18cm rounds.
3 Preheat oven to 220°C/200°C fan-forced.
4 Divide filling equally among rounds; brush edge lightly with egg. Fold pastry over to enclose filling, press edges together to seal. Brush turnovers, both sides, with egg; place on lightly oiled oven trays.
5 Bake, uncovered, about 20 minutes or until pastry is browned and turnovers are heated through.

serves 8
preparation time 15 minutes
cooking time 35 minutes
per serving 21.1g fat; 1635kJ (390 cal)
serving suggestion Serve with homemade tomato sauce.
tip Fresh peas and corn can be substituted. You will need about 500g unshelled fresh peas and 1 large fresh corn cob.

salmon fillo triangles

20g butter
3 green onions, sliced thinly
1 small red capsicum (150g),
    chopped finely
2 tablespoons plain flour
¼ cup (60ml) milk
½ cup (125ml) cream
1 tablespoon lemon juice
1 tablespoon rinsed drained
    baby capers
30g baby spinach leaves
400g can red salmon,
    drained, flaked
4 sheets fillo pastry
50g butter, melted
150g mesclun
200g cherry tomatoes, halved

1 Melt butter in medium frying pan; cook onion and capsicum, stirring, until onion softens. Add flour; cook, stirring, until mixture bubbles. Gradually add combined milk and cream; stir until mixture boils and thickens. Remove from heat; stir in juice, capers, spinach and salmon.

2 Preheat oven to 200°C/180°C fan-forced.

3 Brush one sheet of the fillo with a little of the melted butter; fold in half lengthways. Place a quarter of the salmon mixture in corner of fillo, leaving a 1cm border. Fold corner with filling over to form a triangular shape; continue folding to end of fillo piece, retaining triangle shape. Place triangle on lightly oiled oven tray, seam-side down; repeat with remaining fillo and salmon mixture.

4 Brush triangles with remaining melted butter; bake, uncovered, about 10 minutes or until browned lightly and heated through. Serve salmon triangles with mesclun and tomato.

serves 4
preparation time 15 minutes
cooking time 15 minutes
per serving 30.8g fat; 1843kJ (440 cal)

salmon and vegetables en croute

Croute literally means "crust". En croute can refer to food served in a pastry case, on toasted or fried bread, or, as here, on a piece of puff pastry.

750g piece salmon fillet
¼ cup lemon juice (60ml)
1 tablespoon olive oil
1 sheet ready-rolled
   puff pastry
1 egg, beaten lightly
2 medium carrots (240g)
3 trimmed celery stalks (300g)
250g fresh asparagus,
   trimmed
⅔ cup (160ml) dry white wine
1 cup (250ml) cream
1 tablespoon seeded mustard
1 tablespoon finely chopped
   fresh chives

1 Remove and discard skin from fish; trim edges and cut fish into 8 slices. Combine fish, juice and oil in large bowl; cover, refrigerate 3 hours or overnight.

2 Preheat oven to 180°C/160°C fan-forced.

3 Cut pastry into quarters; place on oiled oven tray. Cut shallow diagonal slashes in pastry, at 1cm intervals, to form grid pattern. Brush with egg; bake, uncovered, about 10 minutes or until browned.

4 Meanwhile, cut carrots and celery into matchstick-size pieces. Halve asparagus. Stir-fry vegetables, in batches, in heated oiled large frying pan until just tender. Cover to keep warm.

5 Drain fish over medium bowl; reserve marinade. Cook fish, in batches, in same pan until browned both sides and cooked as desired. Cover to keep warm.

6 Pour wine and reserved marinade into same pan; bring to a boil, simmer, uncovered, until reduced by half. Add cream and mustard; cook, stirring, until sauce thickens slightly, stir through chives.

7 Place pastry pieces on serving plates, top with vegetables, fish and sauce.

serves 4
preparation time 35 minutes
(plus refrigeration time)
cooking time 30 minutes
per serving 56g fat; 3457kJ (826 cal)

chicken and artichoke parcels

¼ cup dry white wine (60ml)
½ cup water (125ml)
1 trimmed celery stalk (100g), sliced thinly
1 small brown onion (80g), chopped finely
300g chicken breast fillet, chopped finely
1 tablespoon plain flour
½ cup skim milk (125ml)
400g can artichoke hearts in brine, drained, cut into quarters
2 tablespoons finely chopped fresh basil
8 sheets fillo pastry
cooking-oil spray

1 Preheat oven 200°C/180°C fan-forced.
2 Combine wine, the water, celery, onion and chicken in medium saucepan; bring to a boil. Simmer about 5 minutes or until onion is soft and chicken is tender. Stir in combined flour and milk; stir until mixture boils and thickens. Remove from heat; stir in artichoke and basil. Season with pepper.
3 Cut pastry sheets in half crossways; layer four halves together, brushing lightly with water between each layer. Repeat with remaining pastry sheets. Place one quarter of the chicken mixture on one end of pastry; fold in sides. Roll to enclose filling. Repeat with remaining chicken mixture and pastry.
4 Place parcels on baking-paper-lined oven tray; spray with cooking oil. Bake, uncovered, in oven about 15 minutes or until pastry is browned lightly. Serve with mesclun salad, if desired.

makes 4
preparation time 20 minutes
cooking time 25 minutes
per parcel 5.2g fat; 1074kJ (256 cal)

spanakopita

For this recipe, use silver beet, also known as swiss chard, rather than spinach.

1.5kg silver beet, trimmed
1 tablespoon olive oil
1 medium brown onion (150g), chopped finely
2 cloves garlic, crushed
1 teaspoon ground nutmeg
200g fetta cheese, crumbled
1 tablespoon finely grated lemon rind
¼ cup coarsely chopped fresh mint leaves
¼ cup coarsely chopped fresh flat-leaf parsley
¼ cup coarsely chopped fresh dill
4 green onions, chopped finely
16 sheets fillo pastry
125g butter, melted
2 teaspoons sesame seeds

1 Boil, steam or microwave silver beet until just wilted; drain. Squeeze out excess moisture; drain on absorbent paper. Chop silver beet coarsely; spread out on absorbent paper.
2 Heat oil in small frying pan; cook brown onion and garlic, stirring, until onion is soft. Add nutmeg; cook, stirring, until fragrant. Combine onion mixture and silver beet in large bowl with fetta, rind, herbs and green onion.
3 Preheat oven to 180°C/160°C fan-forced.
4 Brush 1 sheet of the fillo with butter; fold lengthways into thirds, brushing with butter between each fold. Place rounded tablespoons of the silver beet mixture in corner of fillo, leaving a 1cm border. Fold corner with filling over to form a triangular shape; continue folding to end of fillo piece, retaining triangle shape. Place on lightly oiled oven trays, seam-side down; repeat with remaining ingredients until there are 16 spanakopita.
5 Brush spanakopita with remaining butter; sprinkle with sesame seeds. Bake, uncovered, about 15 minutes or until browned lightly.

serves 8
preparation time 20 minutes
cooking time 25 minutes
per serve 23.2g fat; 1330kJ (317 cal)
serving suggestion Drizzle a mixture of chopped cucumber and yogurt over the top of the spanakopitas.
tip To prevent fillo drying out, keep it covered with a damp tea-towel until ready to use.

chicken and leek puff pastry squares

40g butter
1 small leek (200g), sliced thinly
2 cloves garlic, crushed
450g chicken breast fillets, chopped coarsely
2 tablespoons cornflour
½ cup (125ml) dry white wine
½ cup (125ml) chicken stock
½ cup (125ml) cream
2 sheets ready-rolled puff pastry
1 egg, beaten lightly

1 Preheat oven to 200°C/180°C fan-forced.
2 Melt butter in large frying pan; cook leek and garlic, stirring, until leek softens. Add chicken; cook, stirring, until chicken is browned lightly.
3 Add blended cornflour and wine to chicken mixture, then add stock and cream; stir until mixture boils and thickens. Reduce heat; simmer, uncovered, 5 minutes. Cool 15 minutes.
4 Cut each pastry sheet in half; place on oiled oven trays. Spoon a quarter of the chicken mixture onto half of one piece, leaving 1cm border; brush edges with egg. Fold pastry over to enclose filling; pinch edges together to seal. Cut two slits in top of pastry square; brush with egg. Repeat with remaining pastry, chicken mixture and egg. Bake, uncovered, about 15 minutes or until browned.

serves 4
preparation time 20 minutes (plus cooling time)
cooking time 25 minutes
per serving 33.9g fat; 2076kJ (496 cal)
tip Uncooked parcels can be frozen, covered tightly, for up to a month. Thaw overnight in the refrigerator before baking.

chicken and corn pie

If you only want to serve a single pie at a time, freeze one uncooked then, when you want the second, bake it while it's still frozen.

1 tablespoon olive oil
1 large leek (500g),
   sliced thinly
2 cloves garlic, crushed
750g chicken mince
150g fresh baby corn,
   sliced diagonally
1 cup frozen peas (160g)
60g butter
¼ cup plain flour (35g)
2 cups milk (500ml)
1 chicken stock cube
¼ cup grated parmesan
   cheese (20g)
¼ cup finely chopped
   fresh flat-leaf parsley
310g can creamed corn
cooking-oil spray
6 sheets ready-rolled
   puff pastry
1 egg, beaten lightly

1 Heat oil in large heavy-based saucepan; cook leek and garlic, stirring, until leek is soft. Add chicken; cook, stirring, until changed in colour. Stir in baby corn and peas.

2 Melt butter in medium saucepan, add flour; cook, stirring, until mixture thickens and bubbles. Gradually stir in combined milk and crumbled stock cube; stir until sauce boils and thickens. Remove from heat; stir in cheese, parsley and creamed corn. Stir into chicken mixture; cool.

3 Preheat oven to 220°C/200°C fan-forced. Spray two 23cm shallow pie dishes lightly with cooking-oil spray.

4 Cut 2 pastry sheets in half; attach 2 halves onto each of 2 remaining whole sheets on adjacent sides to form two large pastry sheets, seal joins together with palette knife. Gently ease large sheets into each dish; trim edges.

5 Divide chicken mixture between pastry shells. Brush edges with egg; place one of each of the remaining pastry sheets over each pie, trim edges then press with fork to seal. Brush top of each pie with egg.

6 Bake pies, covered, 25 minutes; uncover, bake 20 minutes or until pastry is browned.

serves 8
preparation time 15 minutes
cooking time 1 hour
per serve 45.8g fat; 3338kJ (798 cal)
tip If you want to use fresh peas in this recipe, you need to buy 450g of unshelled fresh peas.

21

antipasto puff pastry tartlets

¼ cup (60ml) olive oil
2 cloves garlic, crushed
1 small red capsicum (150g), chopped coarsely
1 small yellow capsicum (150g), chopped coarsely
1 medium zucchini (120g), sliced thinly
2 baby eggplants (120g), sliced thinly
1 small red onion (100g), sliced thickly
100g semi-dried tomatoes
150g baby bocconcini cheese, halved
½ cup (40g) finely grated parmesan cheese
½ cup firmly packed fresh basil leaves
2 sheets ready-rolled puff pastry
⅓ cup (85g) bottled tomato pasta sauce
2 tablespoons bottled tapenade

1 Preheat oven to 200°C/180°C fan-forced.
2 Combine oil and garlic in large bowl. Add capsicums, zucchini, eggplant and onion; toss gently to coat vegetables in mixture.
3 Cook vegetables, in batches, on heated oiled grill plate (or grill or barbecue) until browned lightly and just tender; return to large bowl. Add tomatoes, cheeses and basil; toss gently to combine.
4 Cut pastry sheets in half; fold edges 1cm inward, place on oiled oven trays. Divide sauce among pastry pieces; top with vegetable mixture. Bake, uncovered, in oven about 15 minutes or until browned lightly. Serve tartlets topped with tapenade.

serves 4
preparation time 20 minutes
cooking time 20 minutes
per serving 29.8g fat; 1794kJ (429 cal)

tarragon chicken and leek pies

40g butter
660g chicken thigh fillets,
    chopped coarsely
200g button mushrooms,
    halved
1 large leek (500g),
    sliced thickly
1 tablespoon plain flour
½ cup (125ml)
    dry white wine
¾ cup (180g) sour cream
1 tablespoon dijon mustard
1 tablespoon coarsely
    chopped fresh tarragon
1 sheet ready-rolled butter
    puff pastry
1 egg, beaten lightly

1 Preheat oven to 200°C/180°C fan-forced.
2 Melt half the butter in large frying pan; cook chicken, in batches, until browned.
3 Melt remaining butter in same pan; cook mushrooms and leek, stirring, about 5 minutes or until leek is tender. Stir in flour; cook, stirring, until flour browns slightly. Stir in wine; cook, stirring, until mixture boils and thickens. Stir in chicken, sour cream, mustard and tarragon.
4 Divide filling among four 1½-cup (375ml) ovenproof dishes.
5 Cut four 10cm rounds from pastry. Brush edges with egg; top chicken mixture with pastry. Use a fork to decorate edges; brush pastry with egg. Make small cuts in pastry to allow steam to escape. Bake pies, uncovered, in oven about 20 minutes or until pastry is browned lightly.

serves 4
preparation time 15 minutes
cooking time 45 minutes
per serving 49.3g fat; 2959kJ (707 cal)

tomato tarte tatin

2 large red onions (400g),
  sliced thinly
½ cup (125ml) balsamic
  vinegar
2 cups (440g) raw sugar
12 medium egg tomatoes
  (900g), halved
1 tablespoon water
2 sheets ready-rolled puff
  pastry with canola oil

1 Preheat oven to 200°C/180°C fan-forced.

2 Heat large lightly oiled frying pan; cook onion, stirring, until onion softens. Add vinegar and 1 tablespoon of the sugar to pan; cook, stirring, until onion caramelises.

3 Place tomatoes, cut-side up, in single layer on oven tray; bake, uncovered, in oven about 20 minutes or until softened and browned lightly.

4 Meanwhile, lightly oil eight 10cm pie dishes. Combine remaining sugar with the water in large heavy-based saucepan; stir over low heat to combine. Cook, shaking pan constantly and stirring occasionally, until mixture crystallises. Continue cooking, stirring occasionally until mixture turns to a thick, dark syrup.

5 Divide sugar mixture among pie dishes. Arrange three tomato halves, cut-side down, in each dish; top with onion mixture.

6 Cut four 10cm-rounds from each pastry sheet; top each dish with pastry round. Bake tarts, uncovered, in oven about 15 minutes or until pastry is browned lightly; stand tarts for 2 minutes before turning onto serving plates.

serves 8
preparation time 20 minutes
cooking time 1 hour (plus standing time)
per serving 9.6g fat; 1661kJ (397 cal)
tip Don't worry when the sugar and water mixture turns to dry crystals. It will liquefy and become a toffee-like mixture as you continue cooking.

free-form spinach and ricotta pie

200g baby spinach leaves
2 tablespoons olive oil
1 medium brown onion (150g), chopped coarsely
1 clove garlic, crushed
2 teaspoons finely grated lemon rind
¼ cup loosely packed, coarsely chopped fresh flat-leaf parsley
¼ cup loosely packed, coarsely chopped fresh dill
2 tablespoons coarsely chopped fresh mint
1½ cups (300g) ricotta cheese
2 sheets ready-rolled puff pastry

1 Preheat oven to 240°C/220°C fan-forced.
2 Boil, steam or microwave spinach until just wilted; drain on absorbent paper. Squeeze out excess liquid.
3 Heat oil in small frying pan, add onion and garlic; cook, stirring, until onion softens.
4 Combine spinach, onion mixture, rind, herbs and cheese in large bowl; mix well.
5 Oil two oven trays and place in oven about 5 minutes to heat. Place a sheet of pastry on each tray, divide spinach mixture between sheets, leaving a 3cm border. Using a metal spatula, fold pastry roughly over edge of filling.
6 Bake pies about 20 minutes or until pastry browns.

serves 4
preparation time 10 minutes
cooking time 30 minutes
per serving 36.8g fat; 2184kJ (522 cal)
tip For best results, use a pizza tray with holes in the base – this will cook the pastry evenly.

lamb fillo triangles

2 cloves garlic, crushed
1 teaspoon ground cumin
1 teaspoon ground coriander
¼ teaspoon ground cinnamon
1 tablespoon pine nuts
250g lean lamb mince
2 tablespoons sultanas
1 tablespoon coarsely
    chopped fresh coriander
1 tablespoon coarsely
    chopped fresh mint
16 sheets fillo pastry
cooking-oil spray
1½ cups (420g)
    low-fat yogurt
½ cup finely shredded
    fresh mint

1 Cook garlic, spices and pine nuts in medium heated dry frying pan about 1 minute or until fragrant. Add lamb; cook, stirring, until lamb is browned and cooked through. Add sultanas, coriander and chopped mint; stir until just combined. Cool 5 minutes.
2 Preheat oven to 180°C/160°C fan-forced.
3 Brush one sheet of the fillo lightly with water; layer with second sheet of fillo. Cut lengthways into thirds. Place 1 tablespoon of the mixture in corner of fillo, leaving a 1cm border. Fold corner with filling over to form a triangular shape; continue folding to end of fillo piece, retaining triangle shape. Place on lightly oiled oven trays, seam-side down; repeat with remaining ingredients to make 24 triangles.
4 Spray triangles lightly with cooking-oil spray; bake, uncovered, about 10 minutes or until browned lightly.
5 Serve fillo triangles with combined yogurt and shredded mint.

serves 8
preparation time 30 minutes
cooking time 20 minutes
per serving 5.8g fat; 805kJ (192 cal)

vegetable and fetta free-form tarts

*Allowing the eggplant to stand
a while covered with salt will
help withdraw most of the
vegetable's slightly bitter juice;
it also helps prevent the
eggplant from absorbing too
much oil when it's cooked. Be
sure to rinse the eggplant well
under cold running water to
remove as much of the salt as
possible and to dry it
thoroughly with absorbent
paper before cooking it.*

1 small eggplant (230g),
   chopped coarsely
coarse cooking salt
1 tablespoon olive oil
1 medium brown onion (150g),
   sliced thinly
2 medium zucchini (240g),
   sliced thinly
4 sheets ready-rolled
   shortcrust pastry
¼ cup (65g) bottled pesto
120g piece fetta
   cheese, crumbled
8 cherry tomatoes, halved
1 tablespoon finely chopped
   fresh basil
1 egg, beaten lightly

1 Place eggplant in sieve or colander; sprinkle
all over with salt then stand sieve over sink or
large bowl for 15 minutes. Rinse eggplant well
under cold running water, drain; pat dry with
absorbent paper.

2 Preheat oven to 180°C/160°C fan-forced.

3 Heat oil in large frying pan; cook onion,
stirring, until softened. Add eggplant and
zucchini to pan; cook, stirring, until vegetables
are softened.

4 Using a plate as a guide, cut a 20cm round
from each pastry sheet; place rounds on oiled
oven trays. Spread equal amounts of pesto in
centre of each round, leaving a 4cm border
around the outside edge.

5 Divide vegetables among rounds over pesto;
top each with equal amounts of cheese, tomato
and basil. Fold borders over fillings; brush
around pastry edge with egg. Bake, uncovered,
in oven about 40 minutes or until pastry is
browned lightly.

serves 4
preparation time 30 minutes
(plus standing time)
cooking time 50 minutes
per serving 57.8g fat; 3570kJ (853 cal)

roasted vegetable fillo tart

6 medium egg tomatoes
(450g), quartered
1 small red onion (100g),
sliced thickly
2 small yellow capsicums (300g)
2 small red capsicums (300g)
100g low-fat fetta
cheese, crumbled
1 tablespoon finely shredded
fresh basil
9 sheets fillo pastry
cooking-oil spray

1 Preheat oven to 200°C/180°C fan-forced.
2 Combine tomato and onion in baking dish; roast, uncovered, about 30 minutes or until onion softens.
3 Meanwhile, quarter capsicums; remove and discard seeds and membranes. Roast under grill, skin-side up, until skin blisters and blackens; cover capsicum pieces with plastic or paper 5 minutes. Peel away skin; slice capsicum thinly. Place capsicum, cheese and basil in baking dish with tomato mixture; stir gently to combine.
4 Lightly oil oven tray. Stack sheets of fillo on tray, spraying every third sheet with cooking-oil spray. Carefully fold over all four edges of the stack to create 18cm x 30cm tart "shell".
5 Fill tart shell evenly with vegetable mixture; bake, uncovered, about 15 minutes or until pastry is browned lightly.

serves 6
preparation time 20 minutes
cooking time 45 minutes
per serving 4.4g fat; 450kJ (107 cal)
tip Keep fillo covered with a damp tea towel to prevent sheets from drying out before use.

kumara and pea samosas
with cucumber yogurt

Samosas are Indian savoury deep-fried pastries filled with vegetables or meat, or a combination of both.

1 medium potato (200g),
   chopped coarsely
1 medium kumara (400g),
   chopped coarsely
1 cup (125g) frozen peas
20g ghee
1 medium brown onion
   (150g), chopped finely
1 clove garlic, crushed
2cm piece fresh ginger
   (10g) grated
1 teaspoon ground cumin
½ teaspoon ground coriander
¼ teaspoon garam masala
6 sheets ready-rolled
   puff pastry
vegetable oil, for deep-frying
cucumber yogurt
1 lebanese cucumber (130g),
   seeded, chopped coarsely
1 tablespoon coarsely
   chopped fresh mint leaves
200g yogurt
1 clove garlic, quartered
1 tablespoon lemon juice

1 Boil, steam or microwave potato, kumara and peas, separately, until tender; drain.

2 Meanwhile, heat ghee in medium frying pan; cook onion, garlic and ginger, stirring, until onion is soft. Add spices; cook, stirring, until fragrant.

3 Mash potato and kumara together in large bowl until almost smooth. Add peas and onion mixture; stir to combine.

4 Using a 7.5cm cutter, cut nine rounds from each pastry sheet. Place 1 heaped teaspoon of filling in centre of each round; pinch edges together to seal.

5 Heat oil in wok; deep-fry samosas, in batches, until browned all over. Drain on absorbent paper; serve with cucumber yogurt.

cucumber yogurt Blend or process ingredients until combined.

makes 54
preparation time 1 hour
cooking time 50 minutes
per serving 2.6g fat; 173kJ (41 cal)
tips As an alternative to deep-frying, bake samosas, uncovered, in a moderate oven about 30 minutes or until browned.
Prepare the samosas to the end of Step 4 then freeze until needed. There's no need to defrost them before cooking; simply remove from the freezer and deep-fry (or oven-bake) until browned all over and heated through.

pizza scrolls

2 cups (300g) self-raising flour
1 tablespoon caster sugar
30g butter
¾ cup (180ml) milk
¼ cup (70g) tomato paste
2 teaspoons italian herb blend
100g sliced mild salami,
    cut into thin strips
1 medium green capsicum
    (200g), cut into thin strips
2 cups (200g) coarsely grated
    pizza cheese

1 Preheat oven to 180°C/160°C fan-forced. Grease 19cm x 29cm slice pan.

2 Place flour and sugar in medium bowl; use fingers to rub butter into flour mixture until it resembles coarse breadcrumbs. Stir in milk; mix to a soft, sticky dough. Knead dough lightly on floured surface. Using rolling pin, roll dough out to form 30cm x 40cm rectangle.

3 Using back of large spoon, spread tomato paste all over dough base. Sprinkle herbs evenly over base; top with salami, capsicum then cheese.

4 Starting from one of the long sides, roll dough tightly; trim edges. Using serrated knife, cut roll carefully into 12 even slices; place slices, cut-side up, in single layer, in pan. Bake scroll slices, uncovered, about 30 minutes or until browned lightly.

makes 12
preparation time 20 minutes
cooking time 30 minutes
per scroll 9.7g fat; 870kJ (208 cal)

spiced stone-fruit strudel

2 medium peaches (300g),
  quartered, sliced thinly
2 medium nectarines (340g),
  quartered, sliced thinly
2 tablespoons brown sugar
½ cup (80g) sultanas
1½ teaspoons ground
  cinnamon
½ teaspoon ground nutmeg
⅓ cup (25g) fresh
  breadcrumbs
6 sheets fillo pastry
20g butter, melted
2 tablespoons milk
2 teaspoons icing sugar

1 Combine peach, nectarine, brown sugar, sultanas, spices and breadcrumbs in medium bowl.

2 Preheat oven to 200°C/180°C fan-forced. Grease oven tray and line with baking paper.

3 Stack fillo sheets, brushing all sheets lightly with half of the combined butter and milk. Cut fillo stack in half widthways; cover one stack with baking paper then with a damp tea towel, to prevent drying out.

4 Place half of the fruit mixture along centre of uncovered fillo stack; roll from one side to enclose filling, sealing ends of roll with a little of the remaining butter mixture. Place strudel, seam-side down, on tray; brush all over with a little of the remaining butter mixture. Repeat process with remaining fillo stack, fruit mixture and butter mixture.

5 Bake strudels, uncovered, about 25 minutes or until browned lightly. Cut each strudel in half widthways; divide among plates, dust with sifted icing sugar.

serves 4
preparation time 20 minutes
cooking time 25 minutes
per serving 5.5g fat 1191kJ (285 cal)
tip You can use canned peaches and nectarines if fresh ones aren't available.

blueberry and fillo pastry stacks

4 sheets fillo pastry
cooking-oil spray
125g packaged light
   cream cheese
½ cup (125ml) light cream
2 teaspoons finely grated
   orange rind
2 tablespoons icing sugar
blueberry sauce
300g blueberries
¼ cup (55g) caster sugar
2 tablespoons orange juice
1 teaspoon cornflour

1 Preheat oven to 200°C/180°C fan-forced. Lightly grease two oven trays.

2 Spray one fillo sheet with oil; layer with another fillo sheet. Halve fillo stack lengthways; cut each half into thirds to form six fillo squares. Repeat process with remaining fillo sheets. Place 12 fillo squares onto trays; spray with oil. Bake, uncovered, about 5 minutes or until browned lightly; cool 10 minutes.

3 Meanwhile, make blueberry sauce.

4 Beat cream cheese, cream, rind and half the icing sugar in small bowl with electric mixer until smooth.

5 Place one fillo square on each serving plate; spoon half the cream cheese mixture and half the blueberry sauce over squares. Repeat layering process, finishing with fillo squares; dust with remaining sifted icing sugar.

blueberry sauce Cook blueberries, sugar and half of the juice in small saucepan, stirring, until sugar dissolves. Stir in blended cornflour and remaining juice; cook, stirring, until mixture boils and thickens slightly. Remove from heat; cool 10 minutes.

serves 4
preparation time 15 minutes
cooking time 10 minutes
per serving 13g fat; 1267kJ (302 cal)

apple and rhubarb turnovers

2 medium apples (300g)
20g butter
2 cups (220g) coarsely
   chopped trimmed rhubarb
⅓ cup (75g) firmly packed
   brown sugar
1 tablespoon lemon juice
½ teaspoon ground cinnamon
2 sheets ready-rolled
   butter puff pastry
1 egg, beaten lightly
1 tablespoon icing sugar

1 Preheat oven to 200°C/180°C fan-forced.
2 Peel and core apples; cut into thin wedges. Melt butter in medium frying pan; cook apple, rhubarb, sugar and juice, stirring occasionally, until sugar dissolves and apple starts to caramelise. Stir in cinnamon; cool 15 minutes.
3 Cut two 14cm-rounds from each pastry sheet. Place a quarter of the fruit mixture on each pastry round; brush around edges with egg. Fold pastry over to enclose filling; pinch edges together to seal. Place turnovers on lightly greased oven tray; brush with egg.
4 Bake, uncovered, in oven about 15 minutes or until turnovers are browned lightly. Dust with sifted icing sugar; serve warm with cream or ice-cream, if desired.

serves 4
preparation time 15 minutes
(plus cooling time)
cooking time 25 minutes
per serving 7.8g fat; 885kJ (211 cal)

45

chocolate hazelnut croissants

2 sheets ready-rolled
  puff pastry
⅓ cup (110g) chocolate
  hazelnut spread
30g dark eating chocolate,
  grated finely
25g butter, melted
1 tablespoon icing sugar

1 Preheat oven to 220°C/200°C fan-forced. Lightly grease two oven trays.

2 Cut pastry sheets diagonally to make four triangles. Spread chocolate hazelnut spread over triangles, leaving a 1cm border; sprinkle each evenly with chocolate.

3 Roll triangles, starting at one wide end; place 3cm apart on trays with the tips tucked under and the ends slightly curved in to form crescent shape. Brush croissants with melted butter.

4 Bake, uncovered, in hot oven about 12 minutes or until croissants are browned lightly. Serve croissants dusted with sifted icing sugar; serve warm or at room temperature.

makes 8
preparation time 15 minutes
cooking time 15 minutes
per croissant 17.7g fat; 1153kJ (275 cal)

spiced apple fillo cups

425g can pie apples
½ teaspoon ground cinnamon
¼ teaspoon ground nutmeg
½ cup (35g) fresh breadcrumbs
¾ cup (120g) sultanas
1½ tablespoons caster sugar
4 sheets fillo pastry
30g butter, melted
1 tablespoon icing sugar

1 Preheat oven to 200°C/180°C fan-forced. Grease eight holes of a 12-hole (⅓-cup/80ml) muffin pan.
2 Combine apple, cinnamon, nutmeg, breadcrumbs, sultanas and caster sugar in medium bowl.
3 Place fillo on board; brush one sheet with a little of the butter, then top with another sheet. Repeat brushing and layering with remaining butter and fillo. Cut fillo stack into quarters vertically, then across the centre horizontally; you will have eight pieces. Press one fillo piece into each of the greased pan holes (four holes remain empty during baking).
4 Divide apple mixture evenly among pastry cases. Bake, uncovered, about 10 minutes or until pastry is browned lightly. Using spatula, carefully remove fillo cups from pan; cool 5 minutes on wire rack. Serve dusted with sifted icing sugar.

serves 4
preparation time 20 minutes
cooking time 10 minutes
per serving 7g fat; 1196kJ (286 cal)

pear and frangipane tarts

In this recipe, we used corella pears, which are small pears with a very pale flesh and delicate flavour. Pure maple syrup is the distinctive-tasting dark-brown syrup made from the sap of maple trees; the product called maple-flavoured syrup (also called pancake syrup) is not a good enough substitute for the real thing.

2 corella pears (250g)
1 tablespoon maple syrup
25g butter, melted
1 sheet ready-rolled
    puff pastry
frangipane filling
40g butter
¼ teaspoon vanilla extract
2 tablespoons caster sugar
1 egg yolk
2 teaspoons plain flour
½ cup (60g) almond meal

1 Preheat oven to 180°C/160°C fan-forced.
2 Peel pears; cut in half lengthways. Using small knife, carefully remove core.
3 Combine maple syrup and melted butter in small bowl.
4 Place pear in small baking dish, cut-side down; brush with syrup mixture. Bake, uncovered, about 15 minutes or until just tender; reserve any juice in dish.
5 Meanwhile, make frangipane filling.
6 Cut pastry into four squares; place squares on lightly greased oven tray. Using metal spatula, spread rounded tablespoons of frangipane filling over each square, leaving 2cm border on all four sides. Place one pear half, cut-side down, on each square; fold pastry edge in to form raised border.
7 Brush pear and pastry with reserved juice. Bake, uncovered, in oven about 25 minutes or until browned lightly.

frangipane filling Beat butter, extract, sugar and yolk in small bowl with electric mixer until light and fluffy. Stir in flour and almond meal.

serves 4
preparation time 30 minutes
cooking time 40 minutes
per serving 32.4g fat; 1780kJ (425 cal)
serving suggestion Serve with vanilla ice-cream, if you like.

berry custard pastries

2 sheets ready-rolled
  butter puff pastry
2 tablespoons icing sugar
700g mixed fresh berries
custard cream
300ml thickened cream
300g thick vanilla custard
¼ cup (40g) icing sugar

1 Make custard cream.

2 Preheat oven to 220°C/200°C fan-forced. Grease and line three oven trays with baking paper.

3 Cut one pastry sheet in half. Sprinkle one half with 2 teaspoons of the icing sugar; place remaining half of the pastry on top. Roll pastry up tightly from short side; cut log into eight rounds. Repeat with remaining pastry sheet and another 2 teaspoons of the icing sugar.

4 Place rounds, cut-side up, on board dusted lightly with icing sugar; roll each round into an oval about 8cm x 10cm.

5 Place rounds on trays. Bake, uncovered, about 12 minutes or until pastries are browned and crisp, turning halfway through baking.

6 Place a drop of the custard cream on each of eight serving plates (to stop pastry sliding); top each with a pastry round. Divide half the berries over pastries then top with custard cream, remaining berries and remaining pastries. Dust with sifted remaining icing sugar.

custard cream Beat cream, custard and icing sugar in small bowl with electric mixer until soft peaks form. Cover; refrigerate 30 minutes or until firm.

serves 8
preparation time 40 minutes
(plus refrigeration time)
cooking time 12 minutes
per serving 24.6g fat, 1572 kJ (376 cal)

banana tarte tatin

50g butter
⅓ cup (75g) firmly packed brown sugar
¼ cup (60ml) thickened cream
¼ teaspoon ground cinnamon
3 small bananas (390g), sliced thinly
1 sheet ready-rolled puff pastry, thawed
1 egg, beaten lightly

1 Preheat oven to 220°C/200°C fan-forced.
2 Stir butter, sugar, cream and cinnamon in small saucepan, over low heat, until sugar dissolves; bring to a boil. Reduce heat; simmer, uncovered, 2 minutes.
3 Pour caramel sauce into 23cm pie dish; top with banana slices.
4 Trim corners from pastry sheet to form 24cm circle. Place pastry sheet over banana, ease pastry down into side of dish; brush pastry with egg. Bake, uncovered, in oven about 15 minutes or until pastry is browned.
5 Carefully turn tart onto serving plate; serve immediately.

serves 6
preparation time 10 minutes
cooking time 20 minutes
per serving 17.8g fat; 1241kJ (297 cal)
tip Serve with cream or ice-cream.

honey-coated pistachio and rosewater palmiers

¾ cup (110g) roasted
   shelled pistachios
¼ cup (55g) caster sugar
2 teaspoons rosewater
½ teaspoon ground cinnamon
20g butter
2 tablespoons demerara sugar
2 sheets ready-rolled
   puff pastry
1 egg, beaten lightly
½ cup (175g) honey
1 teaspoon rosewater, extra

makes 32
preparation time 30 minutes
(plus refrigeration time)
cooking time 15 minutes
per palmier 4.5g fat;
382kJ (91 cal)

1 Blend or process nuts with caster sugar, rosewater, cinnamon and butter until mixture forms a coarse paste.

2 Sprinkle board with half the demerara sugar; place one sheet of pastry on the sugar. Using rolling pin, press pastry gently into demerara sugar. Spread half of the nut mixture on pastry; fold two opposing sides of the pastry inwards to meet in the middle. Flatten folded pastry slightly; brush with a little of the egg. Fold each side in half to just meet in the middle; flatten slightly. Fold the two sides in half again so they just touch in the middle, flattening slightly. Repeat process with remaining demerara sugar, pastry sheet, nut mixture and egg. Enclose rolled pastry pieces, separately, with plastic wrap; refrigerate 30 minutes.

3 Preheat oven to 200°C/180°C fan-forced. Lightly grease two oven trays.

4 Cut rolled pastry pieces into 1cm slices; place slices flat on trays about 1.5cm apart. Bake, uncovered, about 12 minutes, turning halfway through cooking time, or until palmiers are browned lightly both sides.

5 Meanwhile, combine honey and extra rosewater in small frying pan; bring to a boil. Reduce heat; simmer, uncovered, 3 minutes. Remove from heat.

6 Add hot palmiers, one at a time, to honey mixture, turning to coat all over; drain on greased wire rack. Serve cold.

honey-almond pastries

1½ cups (240g) roasted blanched almonds
½ cup (110g) caster sugar
1 teaspoon ground cinnamon
30g butter, softened
1 tablespoon orange flower water
8 sheets fillo pastry
100g butter, melted
1 cup (360g) honey
1 tablespoon toasted sesame seeds

1 Preheat oven to 180°C/160°C fan-forced. Grease two oven trays.
2 Blend or process almonds, sugar, cinnamon, softened butter and
3 teaspoons of the orange flower water until mixture forms a paste.
3 Cut fillo sheets in half lengthways then in half crossways; cover fillo
rectangles with baking paper, then with damp tea towel. Brush one fillo
rectangle with melted butter; roll 1 level tablespoon of the almond mixture
into log shape. Place log at short end of fillo rectangle; roll to enclose
mixture, folding in sides after first complete turn. Brush with melted butter.
Repeat with remaining fillo rectangles, melted butter and almond mixture.
4 Place pastries, seam-side down, on trays. Bake, uncovered, about
15 minutes.
5 Meanwhile, bring honey and remaining orange flower water to a boil
in medium saucepan. Reduce heat; simmer, uncovered, 3 minutes.
6 Add hot pastries, in batches, to honey mixture, turning until well
coated; drain on greased wire rack. Sprinkle with seeds; cool completely
before serving.

makes 32
preparation time 45 minutes
cooking time 15 minutes
per pastry 7.8g fat, 594 kJ (142 cal)

glossary

almond meal also known as ground almonds; nuts are powdered to a coarse flour-like texture.

breadcrumbs, fresh usually white bread, processed into crumbs.

capers the grey-green buds of a warm climate (usually Mediterranean) shrub, sold either dried and salted or pickled in a vinegar brine. *Baby capers* are smaller, fuller-flavoured and more expensive than the full-sized ones. Capers should be rinsed well before using.

capsicum also known as bell pepper or, simply, pepper; come in many colours: red, green, yellow, orange and purplish-black. Discard membranes and seeds before use.

cheese

bocconcini walnut-sized, fresh, baby mozzarella; a delicate, semi-soft, white cheese. Spoils rapidly, so keep under refrigeration, in brine, for two days at most.

cream cheese commonly known as Philadelphia or Philly, a soft cow-milk cheese. Also available as spreadable light cream cheese; a blend of cottage and cream cheeses.

fetta salty white cheese with milky, fresh acidity. Most commonly made from cows' milk, though sheep and goat varieties are available.

gorgonzola a creamy Italian blue cheese having a mild, sweet taste.

parmesan also known as parmigiano; a hard, grainy cows' milk cheese.

pizza a commercial blend of processed grated mozzarella, cheddar and parmesan cheeses.

ricotta a sweet, soft, white, cow-milk cheese; roughly translates as cooked again.

chocolate, dark eating made of cocoa liquor, cocoa butter and sugar.

cinnamon dried inner bark of the shoots of the cinnamon tree; available in stick or ground form.

coriander also known as pak chee, cilantro or chinese parsley; bright-green leafy herb with a pungent flavour. The stems and roots are also used in Thai cooking; wash well before chopping. Also sold as seeds, whole or ground; these are no substitute for fresh coriander, as the taste is very different.

butter use salted or unsalted (sweet) butter; 125g is equal to one stick of butter.

cucumber lebanese short, slender and thin-skinned. Has tender, edible skin, tiny, yielding seeds and a sweet, fresh and flavoursome taste.

cumin also known as zeera or comino; has a spicy, nutty flavour. Available in seed form or dried and ground.

curry powder a blend of ground spices used for convenience when making Indian food. Choose mild or hot to suit your taste.

custard powder instant mixture used to make pouring custard; similar to North American instant pudding mixes.

dijon mustard a pale brown, distinctively flavoured, fairly mild french mustard.

eggplant purple-skinned vegetable also known as aubergine.

fennel also known as anise or finocchio. Also the name given to dried seeds having a licorice flavour.

flour

plain an all-purpose flour, made from wheat.

cornflour also known as cornstarch. Wheaten, cornflour is made from the fine starch extracted from wheat, not corn (maize).

self-raising plain flour sifted with baking powder in the proportion of 1 cup flour to 2 teaspoons baking powder.

garam masala a blend of spices based on varying proportions of cardamom, cinnamon, cloves, cumin, coriander and fennel, roasted and ground together.

ghee clarified butter; with the milk solids removed, this fat can be heated to a high temperature without burning.

ginger also known as green or root ginger; the thick root of a tropical plant.

ground also known as powdered ginger. Used as a flavouring in cakes, pies and puddings; cannot be substituted for fresh ginger.

pickled is sold in pieces or sliced, and comes in red and pink varieties packed in a seasoned brine.

italian herb blend a blend of dried herbs including basil, thyme, marjoram, oregano, sage, parsley, garlic and rosemary.

kumara Polynesian name of orange-fleshed sweet potato often confused with yam.

leek a member of the onion family; looks like a giant green onion but is more subtle and mild in flavour.

mesclun a salad mix or gourmet salad mix with a mixture of assorted young lettuce and other green leaves, including baby spinach leaves, mizuna and curly endive.

mince meat also known as ground meat.

nutmeg the dried nut of an evergreen tree native to Indonesia; it is available in ground form or you can grate your own with a fine grater.

oil

cooking-oil spray we used a cholesterol-free cooking spray made from canola oil.

olive made from ripened olives. *Extra virgin* and *virgin* are the best, while *extra light* or *light* refers to taste not fat levels.

vegetable any of, a number of oils sourced from plants.

onion

green also known as scallion or, incorrectly, shallot; an immature onion picked before the bulb has formed, having a long, bright-green edible stalk.

red also known as spanish, red spanish or bermuda onion; a sweet-flavoured, large, purple-red onion.

orange flower water concentrated flavouring made from orange blossoms. Available from Middle-Eastern food stores and some supermarkets and delicatessens. Cannot be substituted with citrus flavourings, as the taste is completely different.

parsley, flat-leaf also known as continental or italian parsley.

pastry

fillo also known as phyllo; tissue-thin pastry sheets purchased chilled or frozen.

puff, frozen ready-rolled packaged sheets of frozen puff pastry. Available from supermarkets.

pine nuts also known as pignoli; not in fact a nut but a small, cream-coloured kernel from pine cones.

pistachio pale green, delicately flavoured nut inside hard off-white shells.

salami cured (air-dried) sausages seasoned with garlic and spices.

silver beet also known as swiss chard, blettes and mistakenly called spinach; a member of the beet family.

spinach also known as english spinach and incorrectly, silver beet.

sugar

brown soft, fine granulated sugar retaining molasses for its characteristic colour and flavour.

caster also known as superfine or finely granulated table sugar.

demerara small, golden-coloured crystal sugar.

icing sugar also known as confectioners' or powdered sugar.

sultanas dried grapes, also known as golden raisins.

tapenade a thick paste made from black or green olives, capers, anchovies, olive oil and lemon juice.

vanilla, extract obtained from vanilla beans infused in water; a non-alcoholic version of essence.

vinegar, balsamic made from the juice of Trebbiano grapes; is a deep rich brown colour with a sweet and sour flavour.

zucchini also known as courgette.

conversion chart

MEASURES

One Australian metric measuring cup holds approximately 250ml, one Australian metric tablespoon holds 20ml, one Australian metric teaspoon holds 5ml.

The difference between one country's measuring cups and another's is within a 2- or 3-teaspoon variance, and will not affect your cooking results. North America, New Zealand and the United Kingdom use a 15ml tablespoon. All cup and spoon measurements are level. The most accurate way of measuring dry ingredients is to weigh them. When measuring liquids, use a clear glass or plastic jug with metric markings.

We use large eggs with an average weight of 60g.

DRY MEASURES

METRIC	IMPERIAL
15g	½oz
30g	1oz
60g	2oz
90g	3oz
125g	4oz (¼lb)
155g	5oz
185g	6oz
220g	7oz
250g	8oz (½lb)
280g	9oz
315g	10oz
345g	11oz
375g	12oz (¾lb)
410g	13oz
440g	14oz
470g	15oz
500g	16oz (1lb)
750g	24oz (1½lb)
1kg	32oz (2lb)

LIQUID MEASURES

METRIC	IMPERIAL
30ml	1 fluid oz
60ml	2 fluid oz
100ml	3 fluid oz
125ml	4 fluid oz
150ml	5 fluid oz (¼ pint/1 gill)
190ml	6 fluid oz
250ml	8 fluid oz
300ml	10 fluid oz (½ pint)
500ml	16 fluid oz
600ml	20 fluid oz (1 pint)
1000ml (1 litre)	1¾ pints

LENGTH MEASURES

METRIC	IMPERIAL
3mm	⅛in
6mm	¼in
1cm	½in
2cm	¾in
2.5cm	1in
5cm	2in
6cm	2½in
8cm	3in
10cm	4in
13cm	5in
15cm	6in
18cm	7in
20cm	8in
23cm	9in
25cm	10in
28cm	11in
30cm	12in (1ft)

OVEN TEMPERATURES

These oven temperatures are only a guide for conventional ovens.
For fan-forced ovens, check the manufacturer's manual.

	°C (CELSIUS)	°F (FAHRENHEIT)	GAS MARK
Very slow	120	250	½
Slow	150	275 – 300	1 – 2
Moderately slow	160	325	3
Moderate	180	350 – 375	4 – 5
Moderately hot	200	400	6
Hot	220	425 – 450	7 – 8
Very hot	240	475	9

index

Are you missing some of the world's favourite cookbooks?

The Australian Women's Weekly cookbooks are available from bookshops, cookshops, supermarkets and other stores all over the world. You can also buy direct from the publisher, using the order form below.

MINI SERIES £3.50 190x138MM 64 PAGES

TITLE	QTY	TITLE	QTY	TITLE	QTY
4 Fast Ingredients		Drinks		Pasta	
15-minute Feasts		Easy Pies & Pastries		Potatoes	
50 Fast Chicken Fillets		Finger Food		Roast	
50 Fast Desserts		Fishcakes & Crispybakes		Salads	
50 Fast Prawns (Oct 07)		Gluten-free Cooking		Simple Slices	
After-work Stir-fries		Healthy Everyday Food 4 Kids		Simply Seafood	
Barbecue Chicken		Ice-creams & Sorbets		Skinny Food	
Bites		Indian Cooking		Spanish Favourites	
Bowl Food		Italian Favourites		Stir-fries	
Burgers, Rösti & Fritters		Jams & Jellies		Summer Salads	
Cafe Cakes		Japanese Favourites		Tagines & Couscous	
Cafe Food		Kebabs & Skewers		Tapas, Antipasto & Mezze	
Casseroles		Kids Party Food		Tarts	
Casseroles & Curries		Last-minute Meals		Tex-Mex	
Char-grills & Barbecues		Lebanese Cooking		Thai Favourites	
Cheesecakes, Pavlova & Trifles		Low-Fat Delicious		The Fast Egg	
Chinese Favourites		Malaysian Favourites		Vegetarian	
Christmas Cakes & Puddings		Mince		Vegie Main Meals	
Christmas Favourites (Oct 07)		Mince Favourites		Vietnamese Favourites	
Cocktails		Muffins		Wok	
Crumbles & Bakes		Noodles			
Cupcakes & Cookies		Noodles & Stir-fries			
Curries		Outdoor Eating			
Dips & Dippers		Party Food			
Dried Fruit & Nuts		Pickles and Chutneys		TOTAL COST £	

Photocopy and complete coupon below

Name _____

Address _____

_____ Postcode _____

Country _____ Phone (business hours) _____

Email*(optional) _____
*By including your email address, you consent to receipt of any email regarding this magazine, and other emails which inform you of ACP's other publications, products, services and events, and to promote third party goods and services you may be interested in.

I enclose my cheque/money order for £ _____ or please charge £ _____
to my: ☐ Access ☐ Mastercard ☐ Visa ☐ Diners Club

Card number | | | | | | | | | | | | | | | | |

3 digit security code *(found on reverse of card)* _____

Cardholder's
signature _____ Expiry date _____ / _____

To order: Mail or fax – photocopy or complete the order form above, and send your credit card details or cheque payable to: Australian Consolidated Press (UK), 10 Scirocco Close, Moulton Park Office Village, Northampton NN3 6AP, phone (++44) (01) 604 642200, fax (++44) (01) 604 642300, e-mail books@acpuk.com or order online at www.acpuk.com
Non-UK residents: We accept the credit cards listed on the coupon, or cheques, drafts or International Money Orders payable in sterling and drawn on a UK bank. Credit card charges are at the exchange rate current at the time of payment.
All pricing current at time of going to press and subject to change/availability.
Postage and packing UK: Add £1.00 per order plus 75p per book.
Postage and packing overseas: Add £2.00 per order plus £1.50 per book. **Offer ends 31.12.2008**